FROM MILD TO WILD, DINOSAURS FOR KIDS

DINOSAUR BOOK FOR 6-YEAR-OLD CHILDREN'S DINOSAUR BOOKS

BABY PROFESSOR
EDUCATION KIDS

Speedy Publishing LLC

40 E. Main St. #1156

Newark, DE 19711

www.speedypublishing.com

Copyright 2017

Some dinosaurs roared and howled, and attacked other dinosaurs with their teeth and claws. Others were happy just eating leaves and fruit. Both kinds lived on our Earth for millions of years, long before humans evolved. Let's meet some wild and mild dinosaurs!

THE WORLD OF THE DINOSAURS

The age of the dinosaurs lasted over 200 million years, and for over 130 million years they were the dominant creatures on dry land. They may have become extinct because of climate change they could not adapt to, along with a catastrophic event like a meteor strike or huge volcanic eruptions pouring toxins into the air (learn about this in the Baby Professor book *What Happens Before and After Volcanoes Erupt?*).

Whatever happened to end the age of the dinosaurs, it happened about 65 million years ago. We only know about dinosaurs through the fossils that scientists called paleontologists dig up.

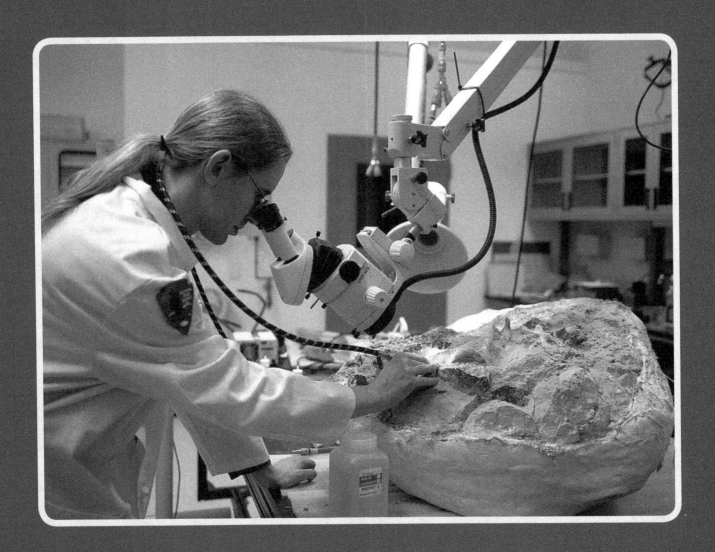

FOSSIL EXAMINATION IN A LABORATORY

SIR RICHARD OWEN

The word "dinosaur" means "terrifying lizard". Sir Richard Owen invented this term in 1842 to describe these ancient animals. Most dinosaurs hatched from eggs and could not fly, a few were comfortable living in water. They are classified as reptiles. One type of dinosaur has a hip structure like lizards, and the other type has hips like those of modern birds. In fact, modern birds are descended from dinosaurs, so you could say that the dinosaurs never became extinct at all!

The largest dinosaurs were more than fifty feet tall and as much as 100 feet long. The smallest ones were about the size of modern chickens.

We are still learning more about dinosaurs. So far, we have identified over 300 species, but we are pretty sure that is nowhere near all the types of dinosaur that once walked the Earth.

DANGEROUS DINOSAURS

Dinosaurs who were carnivores (meat-eaters) were very dangerous to other creatures. They had to kill to get what they needed to eat.

TYRANNOSAURUS REX FACING OFF
AGAINST A TRICERATOPS HERD

THE HUNTING GROUND OF A TYRANNOSAURUS REX

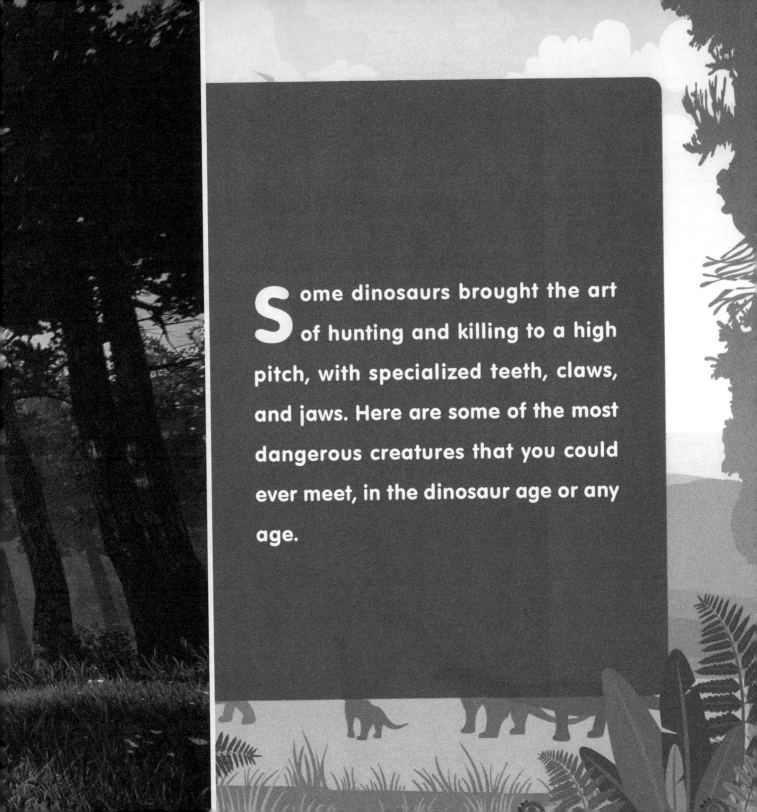

Some dinosaurs brought the art of hunting and killing to a high pitch, with specialized teeth, claws, and jaws. Here are some of the most dangerous creatures that you could ever meet, in the dinosaur age or any age.

SPINOSAURUS AEGYPTIACUS

Spinosaurus was probably the largest type of meat-eating dinosaur, much larger than the T-Rex. It was probably over 50 feet long, and a fast runner. Worse than that, you couldn't even get away by jumping in a lake or the ocean if it was chasing you: this was a dinosaur that knew how to swim. Spinosaurus dominated the northern part of what is now Africa.

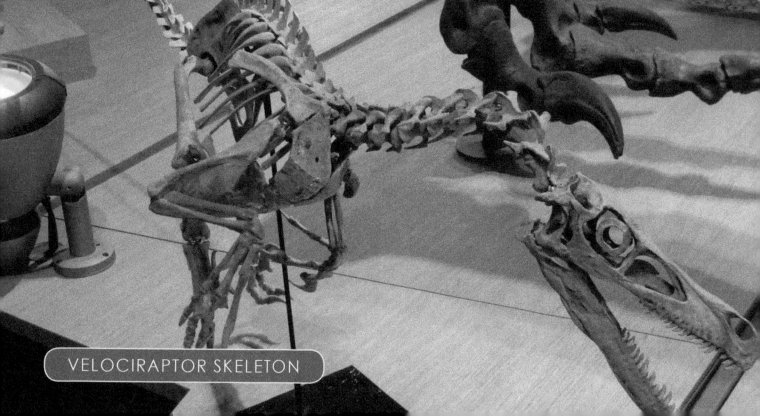

VELOCIRAPTOR SKELETON

VELOCIRAPTOR MONGOLIENSIS

In the *Jurassic Park* movies, velociraptors are the ultimate hunting animal. In reality they were smaller and slower than the movies show. They did have a huge claw like a hook on each foot, and they probably used this hook to help hold down an animal they had attacked while they finished it off with their teeth.

TYRANNOSAURUS REX

This is one of the most famous dinosaurs, and the villain in many scary movies and nightmares. Its bite had three times the force of the jaws of a great white shark.

MAPUSAURUS ROSEAE

This hunting dinosaur grew to over thirty feet long. It probably hunted in packs, working together to bring down much larger plant-eating dinosaurs.

ANKYLOSAURUS MAGNIVENTRIS

Ankylosaurus was a plant eater, but it appears in this list because of its heavy, armored tail. It looks like this dinosaur could beat off an attack by swinging its tail so hard it could break another dinosaur's bones.

ANKYLOSAURUS DINOSAUR

COELOPHYSIS BAURI

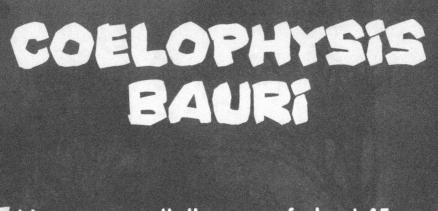

This was a small dinosaur of about 45 pounds, the size of a dog. Like dogs, Coelophysis hunted in packs. They had cutting teeth with very sharp edges and a pack of these animals could attack and bring down very large animals.

MAJUNGASAURUS CRENATISSIMUS

This dinosaur is one of the few that we know that was a cannibal, eating its own children or even other grown members of its species. It had a short, strong snout which probably let it bite and hold its prey until the other animal died, the way modern cats do. `

ALLOSAURUS IN BAŁTOW, POLAND

ALLOSAURUS

Allosaurus was a scary predator of the Jurassic period, as dangerous to other hunters as it was to plant-eating dinosaurs. Paleontologists have found many fossils of other creatures, such as Stegosaurus, with tooth marks from Allosaurus all over their bones.

MEI

This dinosaur, whose name comes from the Chinese word for "deep asleep", was a feathered carnivore. The only example of Mei we have found so far was rolled in a ball, with its tail around its body the way a cat sometimes sleeps. Its head was tucked under one arm. This particular Mei seems to have been buried in a sandstorm in China about 140 million years ago.

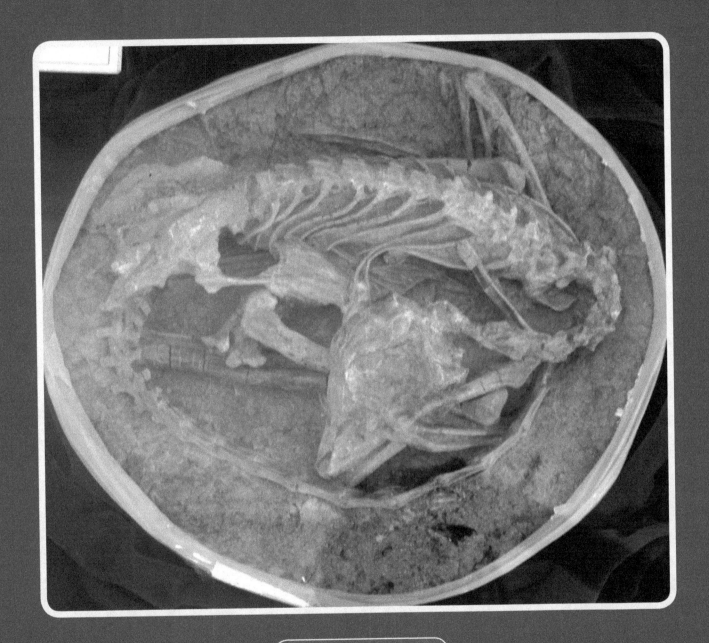

MEI FOSSIL

MILD DINOSAURS

We know nothing about how dinosaurs thought, of course, so we are projecting what we know about grass-eating animals of today, like sheep or cows, when we classify plant-eating dinosaurs as "mild".

Certainly, many of them did not have sharp claws or teeth that would help them survive a battle, so we can guess they mainly fought when they were attacked by dinosaurs that wanted to eat them. On the other hand, even peaceful creatures of today like penguins fight each other to get the best mates and the best nesting places, so "mild" is always a relative term.

However, here are a collection of great beasts from the age of the dinosaurs who were definitely more dangerous to plants than to other living things.

CHAOYANGSAURUS

Chaoyangsaurus was only about three feet long and weighed less than 30 pounds. It had tufts on its tail and stood on its hind legs. It was the ancestor of four-legged dinosaurs like Triceratops, and lived in the late Jurassic and early Cretaceous eras. Chaoyangsaurus probably mainly ate leaves, grabbing nuts and seeds when it could find them. The dinosaur had an odd object on the back of its tail, like a balloon, which may indicate that it was able to swim.

CHAOYANGSAURUS

The thing a bout
Europosaurus
is that trar

EUROPASAURUS

Europasaurus weighed about 1,500 pounds,
Every small compared to its multi-ton
relatives like Brachiosaurus and Apatosaurus.

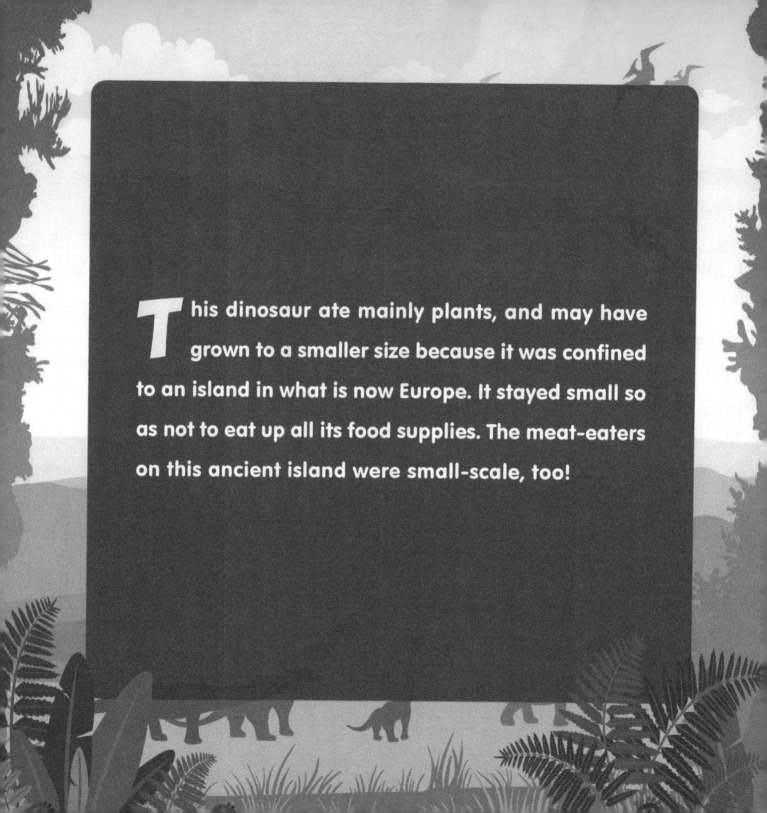

This dinosaur ate mainly plants, and may have grown to a smaller size because it was confined to an island in what is now Europe. It stayed small so as not to eat up all its food supplies. The meat-eaters on this ancient island were small-scale, too!

GIGANTORAPTOR PROTECTING ITS
EGGS FROM TYRANNOSAURUS REX

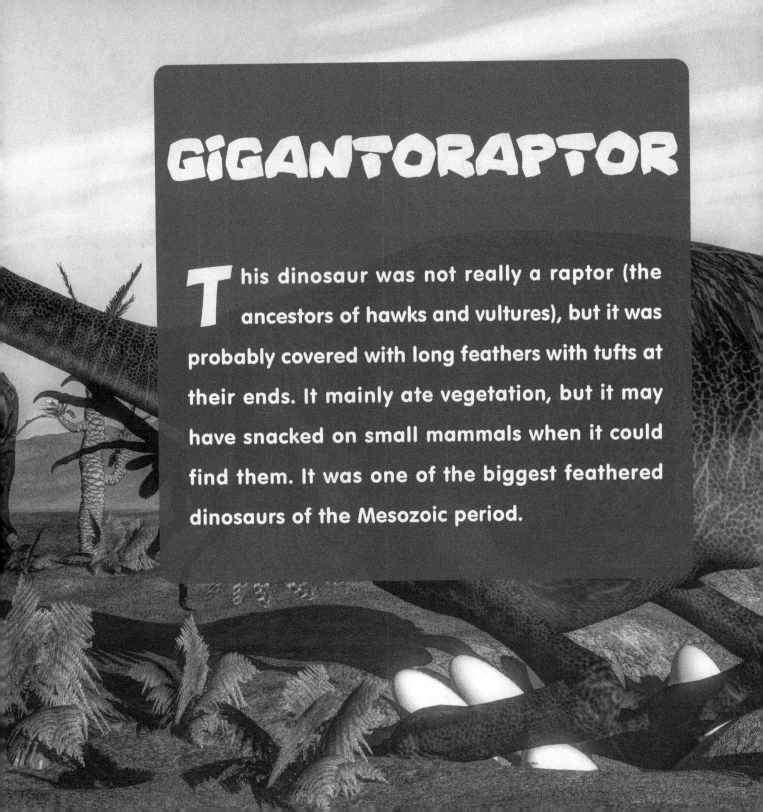

GIGANTORAPTOR

This dinosaur was not really a raptor (the ancestors of hawks and vultures), but it was probably covered with long feathers with tufts at their ends. It mainly ate vegetation, but it may have snacked on small mammals when it could find them. It was one of the biggest feathered dinosaurs of the Mesozoic period.

LEAELLYNASAURA

Leaellynasaura lived in what is now Australia during the Cretaceous period. It was human-sized and had huge eyes, which makes it look cute to us and which probably helped it hunt at night. The dinosaur gets its name from Leaellyn, the daughter of Patricia Vickers-Rich, the paleontologist who found the dinosaur's remains.

LEAELLYNASAURA

LIMUSAURUS INEXTRICABILIS

LIMUSAURUS

Limusaurus was closely related to some of the meat-eating dinosaurs, but the shape of its snout and its lack of teeth suggests this creature preferred grass and flowers. It weighed about 75 pounds and lived in Asia.

MICROPACHYCEPHALOSAURUS

The name for this dinosaur comes from Greek words meaning "the very little lizard with the big, thick head". This creature, with its huge, armored head compared to its size, weighed only about five pounds! It lived in what is now Asia about 80 million years ago.

MINMI

This armored dinosaur lived in what is now Australia, and was built for defense, not attack. It was about ten feet long, weighing about one thousand pounds.

It is remarkable among its relatives for having the smallest brain for its size of any of the ankylosaurs. So even if it wanted to attack you, it probably would not have been able to figure out how to do it!

NOTHRONYCHUS

NOTHRONYCHUS

This feathery, tubby ancestor to birds lived in what is now Mongolia about 80 million years ago. It had long claws for digging, a narrow mouth or beak, and a saggy stomach, and almost certainly lived on seeds and insects.

UNAYSAURUS

Unaysaurus was the ancestor to some of the giant plant-eating dinosaurs that we know better. It lived tens of millions of years before its descendants like the titanosaurs. It was only about eight feet long, and weighed less than 200 pounds, so this ancient dinosaur was just a little bigger than a center on a professional basketball team.

LEARN ABOUT THE ANCIENT WORLD

Dinosaurs dominated the Earth for millions of years, far longer than how long we humans have existed! Find out more about what dinosaurs were like, and why they aren't around any more, in the Baby Professor book *The Big Dino-pedia for Small Learners.*

Visit

BABY PROFESSOR
EDUCATION KIDS

www.BabyProfessorBooks.com

to download Free Baby Professor eBooks
and view our catalog of new and exciting
Children's Books

Printed in the USA
CPSIA information can be obtained
at www.ICGtesting.com
LVHW071557281123
765180LV00012B/263